pro bookmark™

[{ Capturing the riches you read for a lifetime }]

Dr. Roger D. Smith

ProBookmark: Capturing the riches you read for a lifetime

© Copyright 2009, 2012 by Roger Smith. All rights reserved. No part of this book may be reproduced or transmitted in any form or by any means, electronic or mechanical, including photocopying, recording, or by any information storage and retrieval system, without written permission from the author. For information address Modelbenders Press, P.O. Box 781692, Orlando, Florida 32878.

Modelbenders Press books may be purchased for business and promotional use or for special sales. For information please contact the publisher.

PRINTED IN THE UNITED STATES OF AMERICA

Visit our web site at www.modelbenders.com

Designed by Adina Cucicov at Flamingo Designs
Cover image: © Dmitriy Melnikov—Fotolia.com

The Library of Congress has cataloged the paperback edition as follows:

Smith, Roger
    ProBookmark: Capturing the riches you read for a lifetime.
    Roger Smith. – 1st ed.
    1. Reading Skills   2. Study Aids   3. Career Management
    I. Roger Smith   II. Title

ISBN 978-0-9843993-3-8

ProBookmark™

READING IS AN ADVENTURE. It is a journey into new ideas, new hopes, and new knowledge. Reading a book is the same as going on safari in Africa, touring Europe, or cruising the Mediterranean. A book will show you new places, new people, and new ideas. You will learn the history of the world. You will gather knowledge and change your perspective on life. You always come away from a good book changed in some way. Just as a trip to Africa will provide memories and experiences that you will never forget, the time spent inside of a book can create indelible images and change the way you lead your life.

Because reading is so powerful and so important to your life, you should keep a record of your travels. Like carrying a camera or a journal on your tour through Europe, you should come away from the reading of a book with pictures of what you have learned and notes on what you are going to do.

Most people rely on their memory to store everything they have ever read. They hope that the important lessons from a book, or from hundreds of books, will remain with them for years. But, in practice, most of what they read is quickly forgotten. Important information, inspiring stories, and life changing perspectives fade into the mists of their imperfect memories.

ProBookmark™ is designed to change that. These simple pages will help you capture the important information from every book you read. They become a photo album of your travels that you can save for as long as you live and be reminded of the most important ideas you have ever experienced. Like a picture album, each phrase captured on a bookmark triggers a flood of memories, allowing you to relive the treasures that you found in every book.

Don't let another book pass through your hands and your mind without capturing its important ideas so they remain a part of your life forever. Use these bookmarks, save them, and review them to relive the rich treasure of ideas many times over throughout your life.

How to use ProBookmark™

You can look at these bookmarks and understand instantly what you are supposed to do with them. The format is completely self-explanatory.

But here are some tips that will help you get the most out of these powerful tools.

1. **Start at the Beginning.** When you purchase a book, immediately fill out the top of one of these bookmarks. If you wait until you are halfway through the book, then half of the richness of the book will have been lost.

2. **Title, Author, Date, and Topic.** These are the basic facts for categorizing every book. Be sure to fill in the date because you will be surprised at how many years that a really good book will stick with you. It may seem that you read it just last year, when in fact more than five years have passed since you were changed by the book.

3. **Major Message.** In most cases you will not know what the major message of the book is until you are well into it. This section is at the beginning of the bookmark because it is the summary that you will use later to recall the book. Do not try to fill this in first, save it for later or last.

4. **My Rating.** There is a simple 5-star system to rate each book. Color in the number of stars that this book deserves for the pleasure, knowledge, or inspiration that it has given you.

5. **Inspiration.** When the book inspires you to think better thoughts or change your life, capture those ideas right away. Most good books will provide several inspirations for your life.

6. **Action.** We all read books which give us instructions or ideas for taking action in our own lives. Write these down here. This is a small "To Do" list that you want to be sure to remember.

7. **Quotes.** Really good authors have a knack for expressing ideas in words that are powerful and meaningful. Capture those verbatim in this section. You might also note the page on which those gems appear.

8. **Message Tracker.** As you read, keep track of the major points of the book on the back side of the bookmark. This is a map of the story that runs throughout the book. The page numbers will guide you to the really interesting ideas many years after they would have been lost in the paper folds.

9. **Many-to-One.** There is no reason that a book must be summarized onto just one bookmark. Feel free to use two

or three bookmarks to capture the details of an exceptionally powerful book. These are your tools to use in a way that helps you the most.

10. **Improvements.** If you find a way to make these bookmarks more useful to you, please mark them up and let us know. We do not claim to have arrived at the perfect format yet. The form you hold comes from years of revisions. We would be thrilled to hear your ideas on how to make this better. Your suggestion could appear in next year's edition of Pro-Bookmarks™.

Happy reading ... and happy remembering.

From now on, the treasures that lie inside of every book are going to be with you for the rest of your life.

Best Wishes,
Roger Smith

bookmark™

title ....

author .... date ....

topic { ☐ business ☐ health ☐ technology ☐ self-help ☐ leisure ☐ fiction
other ....

major message ....
....
....
.... my rating ☆☆☆☆☆

💡 inspiration ....
....
....
....
....
....

actions ....
....
....
....
....
....

quotes ....
....
....
....
....

page	message tracker

title .... **pro bookmark**™

author .... date ....

topic { ☐ business ☐ health ☐ technology ☐ self-help ☐ leisure ☐ fiction
        other ....

major message ....

....

.... my rating ☆☆☆☆☆

💡 inspiration ....

....

....

....

....

actions ....

....

....

....

....

❝ quotes ....

....

....

....

....

page	message tracker
....	....
....	....
....	....
....	....
....	....
....	....
....	....
....	....
....	....
....	....
....	....
....	....
....	....
....	....
....	....
....	....
....	....
....	....
....	....
....	....
....	....
....	....
....	....
....	....
....	....
....	....
....	....
....	....

title ....   bookmark™

author .... date ....

topic { ☐ business ☐ health ☐ technology ☐ self-help ☐ leisure ☐ fiction
        other ....

major message ....

....

....

.... my rating ☆☆☆☆☆

💡 inspiration ....

....

....

....

....

actions ....

....

....

....

....

quotes ....

....

....

....

....

page	message tracker
....	....
....	....
....	....
....	....
....	....
....	....
....	....
....	....
....	....
....	....
....	....
....	....
....	....
....	....
....	....
....	....
....	....
....	....
....	....
....	....
....	....
....	....
....	....
....	....
....	....
....	....

bookmark™

title ....

author .... date ....

topic { ☐ business ☐ health ☐ technology ☐ self-help ☐ leisure ☐ fiction
other ....

major message ....

....

....

.... my rating ☆☆☆☆☆

💡 inspiration ....

....

....

....

....

....

❗ actions ....

....

....

....

....

....

❞ quotes ....

....

....

....

....

....

page	message tracker

title .... $\boxed{\text{pro}}$ bookmark™

author .... date ....

topic $\Big\{$ ☐ business ☐ health ☐ technology ☐ self-help ☐ leisure ☐ fiction
other ....

major message ....
....
....
.... my rating ☆☆☆☆☆

inspiration ....
....
....
....
....

actions ....
....
....
....
....

quotes ....
....
....
....
....

page	message tracker

title .... probookmark™

author .... date ....

topic { ☐ business ☐ health ☐ technology ☐ self-help ☐ leisure ☐ fiction
       other ....

major message ....

....

....

.... my rating ☆☆☆☆☆

inspiration ....

....

....

....

....

actions ....

....

....

....

....

quotes ....

....

....

....

....

page	message tracker
....	....
....	....
....	....
....	....
....	....
....	....
....	....
....	....
....	....
....	....
....	....
....	....
....	....
....	....
....	....
....	....
....	....
....	....
....	....
....	....
....	....
....	....
....	....
....	....
....	....

title .... bookmark™

author .... date ....

topic { ☐ business ☐ health ☐ technology ☐ self-help ☐ leisure ☐ fiction
        other ....

major message ....

....

....

.... my rating ☆☆☆☆☆

💡 inspiration ....

....

....

....

....

actions ....

....

....

....

....

quotes ....

....

....

....

....

page								message tracker

title .... bookmark™

author .... date ....

topic { ☐ business ☐ health ☐ technology ☐ self-help ☐ leisure ☐ fiction
        other ....

major message ....

....

....

.... my rating ☆☆☆☆☆

inspiration ....

....

....

....

....

actions ....

....

....

....

....

quotes ....

....

....

....

....

message tracker

page	
......	....

title .... bookmark™

author .... date ....

topic { ☐ business ☐ health ☐ technology ☐ self-help ☐ leisure ☐ fiction
other ....

major message ....

....

....

.... my rating ☆☆☆☆☆

inspiration ....

....

....

....

....

actions ....

....

....

....

....

quotes ....

....

....

....

....

page	message tracker

title .... bookmark™ pro

author .... date ....

topic { ☐ business ☐ health ☐ technology ☐ self-help ☐ leisure ☐ fiction
other ....

major message ....
....
....
.... my rating ☆☆☆☆☆

💡 inspiration ....
....
....
....
....
....

❗ actions ....
....
....
....
....

❝ quotes ....
....
....
....
....

page	message tracker
....	....
....	....
....	....
....	....
....	....
....	....
....	....
....	....
....	....
....	....
....	....
....	....
....	....
....	....
....	....
....	....
....	....
....	....
....	....
....	....
....	....
....	....
....	....
....	....
....	....
....	....

title .... bookmark™

author .... date ....

topic { ☐ business ☐ health ☐ technology ☐ self-help ☐ leisure ☐ fiction
other ....

major message ....
....
....
.... my rating ☆☆☆☆☆

inspiration ....
....
....
....
....

actions ....
....
....
....
....

quotes ....
....
....
....
....

page	message tracker

title .... bookmark™

author .... date ....

topic { ☐ business ☐ health ☐ technology ☐ self-help ☐ leisure ☐ fiction
        other ....

major message ....

....

....

.... my rating ☆☆☆☆☆

inspiration ....

actions ....

quotes ....

23

page	message tracker
....	....
....	....
....	....
....	....
....	....
....	....
....	....
....	....
....	....
....	....
....	....
....	....
....	....
....	....
....	....
....	....
....	....
....	....
....	....
....	....
....	....
....	....
....	....
....	....
....	....
....	

title .... bookmark™ pro

author .... date ....

topic { ☐ business ☐ health ☐ technology ☐ self-help ☐ leisure ☐ fiction
        other ....

major message ....

....

....

.... my rating ☆☆☆☆☆

inspiration ....

....

....

....

....

actions ....

....

....

....

....

quotes ....

....

....

....

....

page | message tracker

title .... bookmark™ pro

author .... date ....

topic { ☐ business ☐ health ☐ technology ☐ self-help ☐ leisure ☐ fiction
        other ....

major message ....

....

....

.... my rating ☆☆☆☆☆

💡 inspiration ....

....

....

....

....

actions ....

....

....

....

....

quotes ....

....

....

....

....

page — message tracker

title .... bookmark™

author .... date ....

topic { ☐ business ☐ health ☐ technology ☐ self-help ☐ leisure ☐ fiction
         other ....

major message ....

....

....

.... my rating ☆☆☆☆☆

inspiration ....

....

....

....

actions ....

....

....

....

quotes ....

....

....

....

page	message tracker

title .... bookmark™

author .... date ....

topic { ☐ business ☐ health ☐ technology ☐ self-help ☐ leisure ☐ fiction
        other ....

major message ....
....
....
.... my rating ☆☆☆☆☆

inspiration ....
....
....
....
....

actions ....
....
....
....
....

quotes ....
....
....
....
....

page	message tracker

title .... bookmark™ pro

author .... date ....

topic { ☐ business ☐ health ☐ technology ☐ self-help ☐ leisure ☐ fiction
        other ....

major message ....

....

....

.... my rating ☆☆☆☆☆

inspiration ....

....

....

....

....

actions ....

....

....

....

....

quotes ....

....

....

....

....

page	message tracker

title .... bookmark™

author .... date ....

topic { ☐ business ☐ health ☐ technology ☐ self-help ☐ leisure ☐ fiction
        other ....

major message ....

....

....

.... my rating ☆☆☆☆☆

inspiration ....

actions ....

quotes ....

39

page	message tracker

title .... bookmark™

author .... date ....

topic { ☐ business ☐ health ☐ technology ☐ self-help ☐ leisure ☐ fiction
        other ....

major message ....

....

....

.... my rating ☆☆☆☆☆

inspiration ....

....

....

....

....

actions ....

....

....

....

....

quotes ....

....

....

....

....

| page | message tracker |

title .... bookmark™

author .... date ....

topic { ☐ business ☐ health ☐ technology ☐ self-help ☐ leisure ☐ fiction
        other ....

major message ....
....
....
.... my rating ☆☆☆☆☆

💡 inspiration ....
....
....
....
....

actions ....
....
....
....
....

quotes ....
....
....
....
....

page	message tracker
....	....
....	....
....	....
....	....
....	....
....	....
....	....
....	....
....	....
....	....
....	....
....	....
....	....
....	....
....	....
....	....
....	....
....	....
....	....
....	....
....	....
....	....
....	....
....	....
....	....
....	....

title .... bookmark™

author .... date ....

topic { ☐ business ☐ health ☐ technology ☐ self-help ☐ leisure ☐ fiction
        other ....

major message ....

....

....

.... my rating ☆☆☆☆☆

inspiration ....

....

....

....

....

actions ....

....

....

....

....

quotes ....

....

....

....

....

page	message tracker

title .... bookmark™

author .... date ....

topic { ☐ business ☐ health ☐ technology ☐ self-help ☐ leisure ☐ fiction
       other ....

major message ....

....

....

.... my rating ☆☆☆☆☆

inspiration ....

....

....

....

....

actions ....

....

....

....

....

quotes ....

....

....

....

....

page	message tracker

title .... bookmark™

author .... date ....

topic { ☐ business ☐ health ☐ technology ☐ self-help ☐ leisure ☐ fiction
         other ....

major message ....

....

....

.... my rating ☆☆☆☆☆

💡 inspiration ....

....

....

....

....

❗ actions ....

....

....

....

....

❝ quotes ....

....

....

....

....

page	message tracker

title .... bookmark™

author .... date ....

topic { ☐ business ☐ health ☐ technology ☐ self-help ☐ leisure ☐ fiction
        other ....

major message ....

....

....

.... my rating ☆☆☆☆☆

💡 inspiration ....

....

....

....

....

❗ actions ....

....

....

....

....

❝ quotes ....

....

....

....

....

page	message tracker

title .... bookmark™

author .... date ....

topic { ☐ business ☐ health ☐ technology ☐ self-help ☐ leisure ☐ fiction
        other ....

major message ....

....

....

.... my rating ☆☆☆☆☆

💡 inspiration ....

....

....

....

....

❗ actions ....

....

....

....

....

❝ quotes ....

....

....

....

....

....

page	message tracker
....	....
....	....
....	....
....	....
....	....
....	....
....	....
....	....
....	....
....	....
....	....
....	....
....	....
....	....
....	....
....	....
....	....
....	....
....	....
....	....
....	....
....	....
....	....
....	....
....	....

title .... pro bookmark™

author .... date ....

topic { ☐ business ☐ health ☐ technology ☐ self-help ☐ leisure ☐ fiction
       other ....

major message ....

....

.... my rating ☆☆☆☆☆

💡 inspiration ....

....

....

....

....

actions ....

....

....

....

....

quotes ....

....

....

....

....

page	message tracker

title .... bookmark™

author .... date ....

topic { ☐ business ☐ health ☐ technology ☐ self-help ☐ leisure ☐ fiction
other ....

major message ....

....

....

.... my rating ☆☆☆☆☆

inspiration ....

....

....

....

....

actions ....

....

....

....

....

quotes ....

....

....

....

....

page	message tracker

title .... bookmark™

author .... date ....

topic { ☐ business ☐ health ☐ technology ☐ self-help ☐ leisure ☐ fiction
        other ....

major message ....
....
....
.... my rating ☆☆☆☆☆

inspiration ....
....
....
....

actions ....
....
....
....

quotes ....
....
....
....
....

page	message tracker
....	....
....	....
....	....
....	....
....	....
....	....
....	....
....	....
....	....
....	....
....	....
....	....
....	....
....	....
....	....
....	....
....	....
....	....
....	....
....	....
....	....
....	....
....	....
....	....
....	....
....	....

title .... bookmark™

author .... date ....

topic { ☐ business ☐ health ☐ technology ☐ self-help ☐ leisure ☐ fiction
　　　　 other ....

major message ....

....

....

.... my rating ☆☆☆☆☆

💡 inspiration ....

....

....

....

....

❗ actions ....

....

....

....

....

❝ quotes ....

....

....

....

....

61

page	message tracker

title .... bookmark™

author .... date ....

topic { ☐ business ☐ health ☐ technology ☐ self-help ☐ leisure ☐ fiction
        other ....

major message ....

....

....

.... my rating ☆☆☆☆☆

inspiration

actions

quotes

page — message tracker

bookmark™

title ....

author .... date ....

topic { ☐ business ☐ health ☐ technology ☐ self-help ☐ leisure ☐ fiction
        other ....

major message ....
....
....
.... my rating ☆☆☆☆☆

💡 inspiration ....
....
....
....
....

❗ actions ....
....
....
....
....

❝ quotes ....
....
....
....
....

page	message tracker
....	....
....	....
....	....
....	....
....	....
....	....
....	....
....	....
....	....
....	....
....	....
....	....
....	....
....	....
....	....
....	....
....	....
....	....
....	....
....	....
....	....
....	....
....	....
....	....

title .... bookmark™

author .... date ....

topic { ☐ business ☐ health ☐ technology ☐ self-help ☐ leisure ☐ fiction
        other ....

major message ....

....

.... my rating ☆☆☆☆☆

💡 inspiration ....

....

....

....

....

❗ actions ....

....

....

....

....

❝ quotes ....

....

....

....

....

page	message tracker
....	....
....	....
....	....
....	....
....	....
....	....
....	....
....	....
....	....
....	....
....	....
....	....
....	....
....	....
....	....
....	....
....	....
....	....
....	....
....	....
....	....
....	....
....	....
....	....
....	....
....	....
....	....

title .... bookmark™

author .... date ....

topic { ☐ business ☐ health ☐ technology ☐ self-help ☐ leisure ☐ fiction
        other ....

major message ....

....

....

.... my rating ☆☆☆☆☆

💡 inspiration ....

....

....

....

....

❗ actions ....

....

....

....

....

💬 quotes ....

....

....

....

....

page — message tracker

title .... bookmark™

author .... date ....

topic { ☐ business ☐ health ☐ technology ☐ self-help ☐ leisure ☐ fiction
        other ....

major message ....

....

....

.... my rating ☆☆☆☆☆

💡 inspiration ....

....

....

....

....

❗ actions ....

....

....

....

....

❝ quotes ....

....

....

....

....

page	message tracker
....	....
....	....
....	....
....	....
....	....
....	....
....	....
....	....
....	....
....	....
....	....
....	....
....	....
....	....
....	....
....	....
....	....
....	....
....	....
....	....
....	....
....	....
....	....
....	....
....	....
....	....
....	....

title .... bookmark™

author .... date ....

topic { ☐ business ☐ health ☐ technology ☐ self-help ☐ leisure ☐ fiction
        other ....

major message ....

....

.... my rating ☆☆☆☆☆

💡 inspiration ....

....

....

....

....

✏ actions ....

....

....

....

....

❝ quotes ....

....

....

....

....

page	message tracker

title .... bookmark™

author .... date ....

topic { ☐ business ☐ health ☐ technology ☐ self-help ☐ leisure ☐ fiction
        other ....

major message ....

....

....

.... my rating ☆☆☆☆☆

💡 inspiration ....

....

....

....

....

❗ actions ....

....

....

....

....

❞ quotes ....

....

....

....

....

75

page	message tracker

title .... bookmark™

author .... date ....

topic { ☐ business ☐ health ☐ technology ☐ self-help ☐ leisure ☐ fiction
        other ....

major message ....

....

....

.... my rating ☆☆☆☆☆

💡 inspiration ....

....

....

....

....

actions ....

....

....

....

....

quotes ....

....

....

....

....

page	message tracker

title .... bookmark™

author .... date ....

topic { ☐ business ☐ health ☐ technology ☐ self-help ☐ leisure ☐ fiction
        other ....

major message ....
....
....
.... my rating ☆☆☆☆☆

inspiration ....
....
....
....
....

actions ....
....
....
....
....

quotes ....
....
....
....
....

| page | message tracker |

title .... bookmark™

author .... date ....

topic { ☐ business ☐ health ☐ technology ☐ self-help ☐ leisure ☐ fiction
        other ....

major message ....

....

....

.... my rating ☆☆☆☆☆

💡 inspiration ....

....

....

....

....

❗ actions ....

....

....

....

....

❝ quotes ....

....

....

....

....

page	message tracker

title .... bookmark™

author .... date ....

topic { ☐ business ☐ health ☐ technology ☐ self-help ☐ leisure ☐ fiction
        other ....

major message ....

....

....

.... my rating ☆☆☆☆☆

💡 inspiration ....

....

....

....

....

❗ actions ....

....

....

....

....

❝ quotes ....

....

....

....

....

page	message tracker

title .... bookmark™

author .... date ....

topic { ☐ business ☐ health ☐ technology ☐ self-help ☐ leisure ☐ fiction
        other ....

major message ....

....

.... my rating ☆☆☆☆☆

💡 inspiration ....

....

....

....

....

actions ....

....

....

....

....

quotes ....

....

....

....

....

page	message tracker
....	....
....	....
....	....
....	....
....	....
....	....
....	....
....	....
....	....
....	....
....	....
....	....
....	....
....	....
....	....
....	....
....	....
....	....
....	....
....	....
....	....
....	....
....	....
....	....
....	....
....	....
....	....

title .... probookmark™

author .... date ....

topic { ☐ business ☐ health ☐ technology ☐ self-help ☐ leisure ☐ fiction
        other ....

major message ....

....

....

.... my rating ☆☆☆☆☆

inspiration ....

....

....

....

....

actions ....

....

....

....

....

quotes ....

....

....

....

....

page	message tracker

title .... bookmark™

author .... date ....

topic { ☐ business ☐ health ☐ technology ☐ self-help ☐ leisure ☐ fiction
       other ....

major message ....
....
....
.... my rating ☆☆☆☆☆

💡 inspiration ....
....
....
....
....

❗ actions ....
....
....
....
....

❝ quotes ....
....
....
....
....

page	message tracker

title .... bookmark™

author .... date ....

topic { ☐ business ☐ health ☐ technology ☐ self-help ☐ leisure ☐ fiction
        other ....

major message ....

....

....

.... my rating ☆☆☆☆☆

inspiration ....

....

....

....

....

actions ....

....

....

....

....

quotes ....

....

....

....

....

page	message tracker

title .... bookmark™

author .... date ....

topic { ☐ business ☐ health ☐ technology ☐ self-help ☐ leisure ☐ fiction
        other ....

major message ....

....

....

.... my rating ☆☆☆☆☆

inspiration

actions

quotes

message tracker

page	
....	....

title .... bookmark™

author .... date ....

topic { ☐ business ☐ health ☐ technology ☐ self-help ☐ leisure ☐ fiction
other ....

major message ....

....

....

.... my rating ☆☆☆☆☆

💡 inspiration ....

....

....

....

....

❗ actions ....

....

....

....

❝ quotes ....

....

....

....

....

| page | message tracker |

title .... bookmark™
author .... date ....
topic { ☐ business ☐ health ☐ technology ☐ self-help ☐ leisure ☐ fiction
        other ....
major message ....
....
....
.... my rating ☆☆☆☆☆

💡 inspiration ....
....
....
....
....

actions ....
....
....
....
....

quotes ....
....
....
....
....

page	message tracker
....	....
....	....
....	....
....	....
....	....
....	....
....	....
....	....
....	....
....	....
....	....
....	....
....	....
....	....
....	....
....	....
....	....
....	....
....	....
....	....
....	....
....	....
....	....
....	....
....	....
....	....
....	....

title .... bookmark™

author .... date ....

topic { ☐ business ☐ health ☐ technology ☐ self-help ☐ leisure ☐ fiction
        other .... }

major message ....

....

....

.... my rating ☆☆☆☆☆

💡 inspiration ....

....

....

....

....

❗ actions ....

....

....

....

....

❝ quotes ....

....

....

....

....

page	message tracker
....	....
....	....
....	....
....	....
....	....
....	....
....	....
....	....
....	....
....	....
....	....
....	....
....	....
....	....
....	....
....	....
....	....
....	....
....	....
....	....
....	....
....	....
....	....
....	....
....	....
....	....
....	....
....	....

www.ingramcontent.com/pod-product-compliance
Lightning Source LLC
Chambersburg PA
CBHW031257290426
44109CB00012B/626